MW01121413

Table of Contents

01.1114-10

Copyright

The Complete
Internet Marketing Strategy Guide

© 2010 Executive Coaching - All Rights Reserved

Pre-Release
02-12-11

Executive Coaching
Ed McDonough
Walpole, MA
508-308-8224

www.ExecutiveCoachEd.com
More Time • More Profit • Better Quality of Life!

Executive Coaching
Business Owners
Corporate Professionals

Foreword

The sole purpose of this guide is to present to you the most effective options available for marketing your business through the internet. This does not mean to be successful at marketing via the internet you need to implement every component discussed within.

Instead, based on you, the products and services you offer, and the amount resources you have at your disposal, you can make strategic, intelligent decisions which will allow you to use the internet to your greatest advantage when it is appropriate for you and your business.

The key point I want to make with you is your goal should be to first develop and then implement a "complete" internet marketing strategy which will allow you to maximize your exposure in the shortest amount of time.

Since 2002, I have sold goods and services on the internet using combinations of all but one part of one of the options I'll discuss with you. From a brick and mortar business, to digital online information products, to my consulting, marketing services, project management and business coaching, I can tell you first-hand that you can be successful using the internet to bring more customers to your business. As well as, to regularly keep your business in the mind of your existing customer base.

The internet has become the first place the majority goes to search for the products and services they want to purchase, and beyond a shadow of a doubt, it is here to stay.

I highly encourage you to devour the information in this guide and then develop a common sense, step-by-step, strategic internet marketing plan to make your business more sustainable, profitable and fun in the years to come.

Just So We Are Clear...

Before you head off into what follows, I want to make two things clear.

First, this guide is not a lesson in marketing. To be effective using the internet marketing components outlined within, you first need to **clearly** understand the general principles of effective marketing. There are a ton of online and offline resources (including me) available to help you.

Second, this guide is not about the "How to Do It" it's about the "What to Do". I'm going to give you the details of both the "Must Have" and "Nice to Have" components for successfully marketing on the internet.

How you get them implemented into your marketing strategy is up to you. You can do it yourself, hire folks to help you with certain aspects of it, or acquire the services of someone like me who can oversee the complete project from start to finish, and make sure you get exactly what you want and need, one time and on budget. The bottom line:

Decide what will work best for you, develop a plan and then take the necessary action to implement it in a strategic and timely manner.

I wish you great success!

Ed McDonough

Ed McDonough, CPC
Certified Executive Business Coach

www.ExecutiveCoachEd.com

www.ExecutiveCoachingBusinessBlog.com

The Strategy of Internet Marketing

As you may already know, having a website is not an "Internet Marketing Strategy"; which may be the exact reason you are reading these words.

To begin, **any** effective marketing strategy (i.e. one that actually drives prospects to your business and converts them into paying customers) must be Proactive, Intentional and Consistent.

Let me explain:

- **Proactive**
  Proactive means your marketing campaigns will start based on where your business is now and evolve as your business experience grows. It also means, you stay in-tune with economic environment changes and you pay attention to the growing needs of your customers.

- **Intentional**
  Intentional means that you target a specific demographic with a marketing message which speaks directly to them. This audience should always be the people who are **most likely** to purchase your products and services.

- **Consistent**
  Weekly, Monthly and Quarterly, your marketing happens at regular intervals and never ends. This ensures there are always new prospects being introduced to your business, as well as keeps your current customers (who already know and trust you) in contact with you, and more importantly, on the forefront of their mind.

The Internet Marketing Difference

With traditional print, television and radio advertising, the main goal is to capture the attention of someone who **_may_** be interested in your product or service. In other words, you spend a considerable amount of money for your advertisement, and then you hope (and pray) that the right person, at the right time, will see your ad, emotionally connect to it, and then take action.

It sounds like a long-shot, but it does work. For many years before the internet was invented, people have been marketing their products and services this way and achieving great results.

But today we have a huge advantage over the traditional marketing model.

The most wonderful part of marketing on the internet is people come to it **already focused** on the product or service they are seeking. They come looking for what you have to offer and with the intention of buying.

This gives you a huge advantage because you don't have to try to "capture the attention of someone who **may** be interested". All you need to do is get the right message in front of them when they arrive at your website.

So, the question is:

How do you get the people who are already interested in your product/services to your website?

That's where a *Proactive*, *Intentional* and *Consistent* internet marketing strategy comes into play.

It used to be all you needed was a website which contained the right marketing message and a clear "call to action". But, due to the overwhelming number of websites competing for the same market share, that's changed considerably.

To effectively marketing on the internet today, you need to strategically utilize other key internet marketing components in conjunction with your website. Social Media, Email Marketing, Blogging, Search Engine Optimization and Keyword Specific Websites are all requirements of a sound Internet Marketing Strategy.

In addition, if you really want to step-up to the plate and have your business recognized above the competition, other components such as Online Article Marketing, Podcasts, Video, Internet Radio and having a Mobile Friendly version of your website are extra ways to make your marketing message stand out above the rest and reach a larger audience.

There are also ways to pay to have targeted traffic reach your website in a consistent and timely manner. Pay-Per-Click (PCP) advertising campaigns allow you to have your ad seen by your specific target audience any time you want.

In summary, there are many things you can do to get your website, and in turn, your marketing message seen by the people who are most likely to purchase your products and services, exactly when they are ready to take action.

So, my question to you is:

> *Will aimlessly go off and try one thing after another hoping to be successful, or will you develop a strategic plan for success in advance?*

The Big Picture

Here's the big, high-level picture. It contains all the components we'll cover in detail in the following sections. Keep this picture posted on your wall in plain site as you develop your Complete Internet Marketing Strategy. You can use the following link to download and print it: **http://CompleteInternetMarketingStrategy.com/BigPicture**

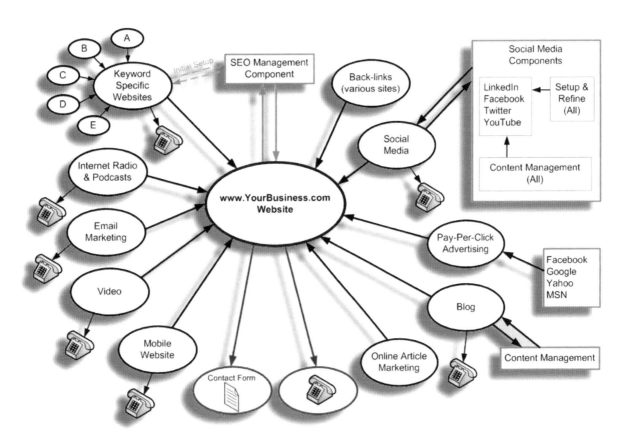

What Every Internet Marketing Strategy Must Have

It's probably no surprise to you that every successful business has a "search engine friendly" website as part of their overall marketing strategy. In addition, they use Social Media, Blogging and Email Marketing to keep in constant communication with their customers and prospects.

The following components are the success essentials which need to be included in your online marketing strategy.

Your Website

The central hub of your Internet Marketing Strategy, your website is the foundation on which your plan will be built. It is vital to your success that you clearly understand how to use this tool to maintain and grow your business.

Three Parts Equal One

Every website has three parts:

The Domain Name:
This is your website address, also known as your URL (Uniform Resource Locator). The best domain name to have is one that exactly matches (or closely matches) your business name or branding model. I highly suggest you select a .com domain for your business if you are located in the United States.

Domain names are not owned, but rather they are registered (think of it as leasing) in as little as one year increments to one person (or business) at a time. When the registration period is over, the current owner has the first option to renew it. In many cases the renewal happens automatically but if it does not, the domain may be registered by someone else.

The Content:
The content is contained within the web pages located under your domain name. Every website must have at least one webpage which is typically called the Home Page.

The content is where the journey begins for your customers and prospects. It contains your marketing message, how to contact you, information about you and your business, and a multitude of other items (such as a place to buy your stuff online) which contribute to your internet presence.

The Host:
Although it may not seem this way in cyberspace, every website needs a physical place to live. This place is often referred to as your ISP (Internet Service

Provider). Somewhere in a data center there is a computer connected o the internet whose only function is to run the software which allows the content of your website to be seen by anyone who types in your URL. There's actually a lot more to the technical side of it than that, but as a business owner, this is really all you need to know.

Therefore, it takes all three parts to have a website. If you already have a website up and running, you are all set with this part.

If you don't have a website, you'll need to register your domain name and acquire a hosting service (ISP). I highly recommend Blue Host (www.BlueHost.com) as they allow you to register your domain name for free, forever, allow you have an unlimited number of websites along with zero restrictions on hosting space and file transfers.

It's the company I used to host all of my websites (over 30 as of December, 2010). You can learn more at the Blue Host website by visiting: **www.BlueHost.com**

Are You Selling or Telling?

So, you have a website, what now?

There are, from a high level perspective, basically two types of websites used by the *small business owner*. This excludes search engine websites (like Google, Yahoo, Bing, et cetera) and ecommerce websites (like Amazon, eBay, Overstock, et cetera). :

The Online Brochure:
This type of site is like a company brochure which has been put online. Its main function is to communicate information about you and your business. It should clearly tell your prospective customers who you are, what you do, why you do it, as well as be a place your existing customers can visit to browse the latest news and information, and/or get online help and support. It of course, should also contain your contact information and the best way to reach you.

The Sales Page:
The sales page website typically contains a marketing message which directly sells a product or service. You can think of it as an online ad which uses a whole webpage to sell rather than inform.

In other words, when someone reaches this page, your marketing message leads through an intentional process which causes them to "take action" right then and there. That action could be to place an online order, complete a contact form, sign-up for your newsletter, register to receive a free downloadable information product, or pick up the phone and call you. Typically it is one page with one "call to action" on it.

Which Do You Need?

To have an Internet Marketing Strategy which is proactive, intentional and consistent, frankly you need both.

Why?

Because people gather information and buy things in different ways. Some people are impulse buyers and when lead to the right Sales Page, with the right marketing message, they will pull the trigger and fulfill the "call to action" you desire right there on the spot.

Other people need more time and information before they will take the next step. The average person will visit a website between 7 and 12 times before they take _any_ action.

Therefore, with most business models, it makes good sense to have both types. I'll tell you a bit more about the best way to accomplish this, and the logistics behind it, in the "Keyword Specific Websites" section below.

For now, let's move on to what you tell you visitors once they get there.

The Masterful Marketing Message

Your marketing message should lead the visitor to follow a concise process. If your site is a "Brochure" style webpage, then it should be easy for people to find exactly what they want.

Ease of use and locating information is many times more important than flashy and fancy. After all, the visitor is there to get information, verify who you are, learn about what you have to offer and find out how to contact you.

If your site is a "Sales Page" style webpage, you need to lead the person through the complete buying experience. The same way an infomercial does.

You show them what problem you can solve, how great their life will be once the problem is solved, why your product or service is the best one to solve the problem, and then how they go about getting it (your "call to action").

Either way, the message you place in front of the visitor has to be concise, easy to use and logical. Make it difficult for them to get what they want, and they will be gone in less than an instant.

In addition, you want your marketing message to be congruent in all your online and offline marketing material. You want your customers to always see and hear the same message no matter what type of media the message is coming from - on your website, in your Social Media, on your Blog, in your videos and podcasts, in your emails as well as in your print, television and radio advertising.

The last part to this section is *why you should tell your visitors why*.

Tell Them Why

One area which is greatly overlooked by most enormous, big, medium, small and single owner businesses is stating up-front WHY you do what it is you do. In other words, the underlying reason why you are in business (and, here's a hint, it's not to make money).

In his book, "Start With Why", author Simon Sinek says, "People don't buy WHAT you do, they buy WHY you do it".

He goes on to explain that most companies miss the boat because they only communicate WHAT they do and HOW they do what they do to their customers and prospects. But, he states, the companies that clearly tell people WHY they do what they do, excel on all levels.

It's an extremely intriguing concept I encourage you to explore. I've posted a video by Simon on my blog which reveals the benefits to clearly identifying WHY you are in business and telling everyone about it.

You can watch this video by visiting:

http://ExecutiveCoachingBusinessBlog.com/ExecutiveCoaching/startwithwhy

Keyword Specific Websites

In regards to internet marketing, a keyword is a word or phrase which relates to a specific product, service or company name.

When it comes to searching for things on the internet, many times the search term (the words you type into the search box on, for instance, Google) and the keyword (or keyword phrase) are one in the same.

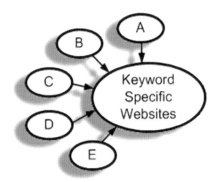

For example, let's say you live in Boston, Massachusetts and you are looking to buy some furniture. You could open Google, type the word **"furniture"** in the search box and click on search. The results you'll receive will be widely varied because the "search term" you typed in isn't very specific.

So let's narrow the search down. In this case you're looking for a really nice piece of furniture so you decide you want something custom made. Now your Google search term becomes **"custom furniture"** and gives you a more refined set of results.

You could take it down even more by using the search term **"custom furniture boston"** which would give you very precise results in your local area. In other words, Google will display the most relevant websites based on the search term you use; in this case, websites from businesses in Boston who sell custom furniture.

How this works is, Google has a list (called a website index) of just about every website known to mankind. When you search, Google matches the terms in the search box with the terms in the website index so it can display the most relevant websites. In reality, there's a lot more to it than that, but I think you can see how this works from a high level.

On the Flip Side...
Now let's take a look at this from the perspective of the business.

Let's say your Boston based business is called *Hey Now furniture,* which sells custom furniture, and your website is www.HeyNowFurntiure.com. The name of your website is perfect because it matches your business name exactly (good job!).

Now, although people who already know about your business may use the search term "hey now furniture" to find your website (and business), you also know people who don't know about your business are out there searching using the keyword "custom furniture boston".

This is where Keyword Specific Websites are a useful marketing tool.

In this example, if you had registered the domain name *CustomFurnitureBoston.com* you could have an additional website located at this address which exactly matches the keyword people are searching on.

This additional site would show up very high in Google (probably in the top ten on the first page of the results) when someone used that specific search term. This "keyword specific" website would lead the visitor to your main website (www.HeyNowFurntiure.com) allowing them to find you through a search engine but in another way.

Again, I want to mention there's a lot more to using and setting up Keyword Specific Websites than that, but I think you can see how this works from a high level.

Which Keywords Do You Use?

Now the question is: Which keywords do you use to setup your additional websites?

First, it is probably obvious that you want to base your Keyword Specific Websites on keywords people actually use when searching the internet.

For instance using our furniture business example, people do search for furniture using the keyword "custom furniture boston". However, people do not search for furniture using the keyword "handmade furniture boston", therefore this may not be a good domain name to use for a Keyword Specific Website.

So how do you know what keywords are used?

There are many ways to determine which keywords are most used in searches. The best place to start is within Google using their free Keyword Tool.

Google occasionally changes the location of this tool within their website, so you may need to search on it if the following link doesn't work.

Try this: **https://AdWords.Google.com/select/KeywordToolExternal**

What Goes On the Keyword Site?

Each keyword specific website should be optimized to be search engine friendly (we'll talk about that next) and for the specific keyword/domain name being used.

The site, at minimum, should contain a link to your main website, your contact information and information about your business based on the keyword being used. It can be also be a "Sales Page" for a specific product or service you sell, the choice is up to you.

Keyword Specific Website Examples

When I did a search on "executive coaching" using the Google keyword tool, two of search terms that came up which folks actually use to search were, "executive coaching boston ma" and executive coaching companies".

Both of these domain names were available so I register them and then had a "Brochure Style" keyword specific website created and uploaded.

You can see them here:

> **www.ExecutiveCoachingBostonMA.com**

> **www.ExecutiveCoachingCompanies.com**

Notice the intention of these websites is to give people more information about me and how I can help them. The action I want them to take is either call me or request more information through my online form.

SEO – Search Engine Optimization

Search Engine Optimization is a process by which a series of modifications are made to the pages of a website so as to increase its visibility (or position) when searched for through a search engine (such as Google, Bing or Yahoo).

The modification (or optimization) of a website may involve editing its visible content as well as the underlying "code" (often referred to as HTML) to both increase its relevance to specific keyword search phrases and increase the ranking in the search engine index.

A properly optimized webpage will be listed in the top ten organic search engine results for the specific keywords it is optimized for.

Note: Organic search results refer to the items listed on the left side of the search engine page; paid advertisements on the right side of the page. More on this in later in the "Pay-Per-Click Advertising" section.

How Important Is It to Your Business?

There are many different philosophies, tactics and strategies regarding Search Engine Optimization.

A common misconception is that it is a onetime event. To some degree this is true. There are many modifications during the initial optimization which happen once.

However, based on your type of business and what you are trying to accomplish with your website, an ongoing SEO strategy may be the only thing that keeps your website at the top of the organic search engine results, and in turn, in front of your customers.

Search Engine Optimization is a critical part of getting your message in front of your target market. If people who are searching for your products and services cannot find your webpage, then they will not find you.

Here's the bottom line: If you are looking to increase your revenue based on people coming to your website and taking action, then part of your proactive, intentional and consistent internet marketing strategy must include some level of ongoing Search Engine Optimization.

Another way to view this is, before a potential internet customer can take action towards using your products and services, they need to get to your website.

This means your website must be "search engine friendly" so it can be quickly and easily found. One of the best ways to accomplish this is through properly optimized web pages which are reviewed and updated regularly.

Another point worth noting is SEO is not static. For instance, it's not just a list of "X" number of things that get done and it ends there.

As the search engines (specifically Google) continue to change the way they index and rank web pages (called an algorithm), SEO tactics and strategies need to evolve along with it. This is another reason why it is important for you to have a consistent SEO strategy in place.

Social Media Marketing

In this document, *Social Media* refers to websites which allow "social interaction" between users in a given online community. Through web-based technology, community members engage in interactive dialogue as well as exchange and share online content.

Examples of these websites are Twitter (www.twitter.com), Facebook (www.facebook.com) and LinkedIn (www.linkedin.com), all which are free to join and use.

Social Media Marketing utilizes these social platforms as a marketing tool. The goal is to deliver a consistent stream of friendly, useful content which the users will share with their friends (and contacts), and in turn help a company increase their brand exposure and broaden their reach to prospective customers.

In addition, Social Media Marketing channels can benefit the business and user community by providing another channel for customer support, a means to gain customer insight, and a method of managing the business's online presence and reputation.

Social Media Marketing Etiquette

What Social Media Marketing should <u>not</u> be mistaken for is a way to continually "push" special offers and advertisements in front of the audience. In reality, this type of strategy will have a huge negative effect and ultimately result in lost revenue.

The key factor to successfully using social media as one of your internet marketing tools is to fully grasp the concept that a relationship with the audience must be built prior to the start of any type of marketing.

This means a two-way dialogue needs to take place between the business and the user community. A conversation which is not about the products and services you offer yet is very relevant to the line of work you are in.

Discussions, high-level advice and the exchange of ideas are a few of the methods to get the user community to interact in a fun and enlightening way while letting them know you are the expert in the field.

Trust and integrity are essentials to always keep in mind as you market your products and services, and this is especially true for Social Media Marketing.

Getting the "public" to freely talk about your business (and you) in a positive light online is one of the most powerful ways to drive up sales and revenue. Being pushy and self-centered will have the opposite effect and most likely to a greater order of magnitude.

Understanding and implementing an intentional and consistent Social Media Marketing strategy can have a huge positive impact on the reputation of you, your business and the revenue.

It is a corner stone for marketing your products and services online and must be considered a top priority in your internet marketing strategy.

Making the Connection

One of the big questions I constantly hear from business owners is how long will it take to make a solid connection with my audience through a social media platform. In other words, they want to know how much time and effort it will take in order to get a return on their investment.

Unfortunately there is no "fixed" answer. The reason is, the "connection time" varies from industry to industry, it is proportional to the frequency in which the social platform is updated, and it is based on the content being used to reach the audience along with its ability to keep them engaged.

Most business owners do not want to assume the cost of having someone else manage and update their Social Media platforms so they take the task on themselves and squeeze it in whenever possible. This usually leads to very poor results and a lot of wasted time.

Businesses that either dedicate their own personnel, or hire a Social Media consultant, experience the greatest outcome. This is because it takes a very consistent and deliberate strategy to be effective.

In general, each platform should be updated several times on a daily basis. Initially, the focus is on building rapport by engaging the community in an ongoing dialogue. After some period of time, once the community is of a substantial size and has shown its loyalty, proactive, strategic marketing can begin.

Making the connection is truly based on time, effort, content and budget. The better the strategy you have, the better the results you'll get.

Backlinks

A backlink is best defined as a link to your website from another website. In other words, they are links which when clicked on direct a user to your website from some other website. This is also known as an inbound or incoming link.

One of the most significant reasons to have backlinks lies in Search Engine Optimization because the number of backlinks is one indication of the popularity (or importance) of your website against all others.

For instance, the numbers of backlinks to a website are used as part of the Google algorithm to determine the site's Page Rank. The better the Page Rank, the higher it will be displayed for a given keyword search.

In addition, the backlinks to a webpage may be of significant personal, cultural or semantic interest because they indicate who is paying attention to you and your website. Typically this is not as important as your Page Rank, but nonetheless, it is important.

An essential part of your Internet Marketing Strategy is to get your website listed (and linked) in as many relevant directories as possible so it shows up higher in the organic search results. In addition, it is also a good idea to get your website link placed on other business sites which provide complementary services and products.

Blogging

The term Blog is the concatenation of the phrase "web log". A blog is typically part of a website in which the author regularly provides commentary, descriptions of events, or other forms of media such as graphics, audios or videos. In most cases, the blog subject matter generally revolves around a particular topic of theme.

The entries (known as posts) are commonly displayed in reverse-chronological order and made by one or more of the blog administrators (the author); this is the act of blogging.

Most blogs are configured to be interactive, allowing visitors to leave comments in response to a particular post. This interactive capability is important as it allows the author to build a community of readers who share the same ideals and philosophies.

From a marketing standpoint, this is another exceptional tool for building online relationships with people. Readers will not only loyally read your blog as you update it, they will readily forward, link to and pass your posts onto others.

It's important to remember, people are more likely to conduct business with someone they know and trust, and someone who shares the same values as they do.

Types of Blogs

In general, there are two types of blogs; they are Non-Hosted and Hosted.

A Non-Hosted blog runs on the website which contains (hosts) the blogging software (or program). Although there are many free blogging sites to choose from, currently WordPress (Wordpress.com) is the one most recommended.

There is no cost to setup a blog (or website) hosted on WorPress.com. The software is as sophisticated as it is easy to use and they allow you to customize your WordPress URL.

Here's an example of a Non-Hosted WordPress site:
http://ExecutiveCoachEd.wordpress.com

A Hosted blog typically resides on your website server (your ISP). This means the blogging software has to be installed on the server before the blog can be setup. Many ISPs, such as www.BlueHost.com, have a special arrangement with WordPress so they offer a "one click" installation of the program. This makes it a snap to get the software installed in a matter of minutes.

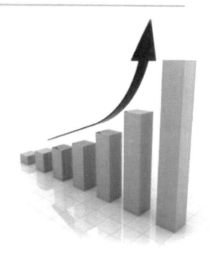

The benefit to a hosted blog is that in can be setup to run from within your existing website or using a unique domain name and URL. In addition, if you want to have your WordPress blog/site customized by a website designer, having a hosted site offers greater flexibility.

Here's an example of a Hosted WordPress blog:
http://ExecutiveCoachingBusinessBlog.com

Blogging Frequency

Unlike the frequency of Social Media the rate at which one blogs is considerably much less. The shortest and most common interval is once a day, which is highly recommended to keep your audience fully engaged.

The maximum interval is once a week. Any interval which is greater than this will not yield effective results over a long period of time.

Blog Themes

Before you setup your blog and start adding content, it's important to determine your blogging strategy or theme. In other words, you need to determine what value your blog will give the reader.

You should keep in mind, the reason to operate a blog is to engage the audience in a regular dialogue and build lasting rapport. It should not be used as a direct sales tool. Again, you want people to get to know you, understand your values and trust you.

Here are several types of blog post themes you can use.

- Informational: This is one of the more common blog posts; you simply give information on a specific topic or subject matter.

- Instructional: These are posts which tell people how to do something. This is one of the best blog themes and most popular types because people search the internet to learn "how to" do things.

- Lists: Lists are one of the easiest ways to write a post and are usually very popular with readers. In addition, it's a great way to get people and other bloggers to share your information. Ideas you can use for list are: "7 Ways to…"; "The Top Ten Reasons Why…"; "9 Ways to Improve…"; and so on.

- Reviews: Often when a person is considering buying a new product, they will search for a review on it first and because of this the word "review" is a highly searched for term. You can review products or services on your blog as a way to help your readers make more intelligent buying decisions.

- Interviews: These can be written, audio or video. Simply find a Subject Matter Expert on the topic you want to create a discussion on, ask some useful pointed questions and let the expert provide the content.

- Video and Podcasts: Outside of interviews as previously mentioned, posting links to some of your favorite podcasts and videos is another way to deliver great content to your readers without having to create it from scratch. For example www.Ted.com is a good resource for video. Note: TED is a small nonprofit devoted to "Ideas Worth Spreading".

- Profiles: A profile posts focuses on a particular person or like-minded expert who shares your niche market in some capacity. You simply select an interesting personality (pertaining to your blog's overall subject), do a little research on them and then to present your findings to your readers.

- Link Posts: This is a very simple method of providing valuable content to your readers. When you find a relevant, good quality post on another website or blog, you write an explanation of why you're recommending it and then provide a link to it.

- Inspirational: Here you give advice and/or tell a motivational success story with the goal of inspiring your readers. Contrary to what is on the evening news, people like to hear "good news stories" as it inspires them to persist with what they are doing and going through.

These are just a few of the more common types of blog post themes you can model. There are many more which include, but are certainly not limited to, "Problem" Posts, Contrasting Opinions, Rants, Research, Prediction and Review Posts, Critique Posts, What If (or Hypothetical), Debate, Satirical, Project Posts, Polls, Quiz Posts, et cetera.

Also keep in mind that you are not limited to a specific number of these. A blog which continually has the attention of its readers will make use of as many of these themes as possible.

Email Marketing

Email marketing is a form of Direct Marketing which uses electronic mail as a means of communicating with the audience. It is sometimes referred to as "push" marketing because the information is pushed out to the target market by the business.

Email can serve many purposes however from a marketing perspective it is typically used to acquire new customers or convince current customers to purchase additional goods and services.

Some business use email strictly as a way to push out limited-time special offers. Others incorporate their offers and general advertisements into a newsletter (also known as eZine) which goes out periodically (i.e. weekly). In essence, every e-mail sent to a prospect or customer could be considered email marketing if it contains some sort of marketing message.

A business considering the use of email marketing must make sure their program does not violate spam laws such as the US CAN-SPAM (Controlling the Assault of Non-Solicited Pornography and Marketing) Act of 2003. Spamming violations can get your business Blacked Listed on the internet and your email blocked for an indefinite period of time.

Establishing an Effective Campaign

United States firms spend millions of dollars a year on email marketing however the numbers are sketchy as to the return on investment.

There are two components which have a major effect on the success of an email campaign:

1. **Getting the Mail Delivered**
   Anti-spam software and email filters make it nearly impossible for unsolicited email to reach the intended recipient. If they don't know it's coming, it probably will not make it to their inbox.

2. **Getting the Reader to Take Action**
   Once the email is received and opened, the next task is to get the reader to take action. If there is no compelling benefit immediately apparent to the reader, chances are it will wind up in the Trash Folder.

Studies show well planned email campaigns will have an approximate delivery rate of 56 percent. Out of these 56% of emails which are delivered, about 13 percent of the readers will take the next step towards making a purchase.

The only way to effectively know how well your email campaigns are doing is to have a means of measuring the results. There are many top online email marketing services which will provide you with the necessary tools and statistics you need to run successful campaigns.

These services allow you to easily track and measure your delivery and open ratios as well as your click-through (the process of clicking a link in the email to a website or order form) rate. Along with many others, these statistics will permit you to measure the effectiveness of your campaigns and validate that the content of the email is getting the call to action you desire.

In addition, email that comes from one of the top email services providers is typically seen as an "accepted communication" and allowed through spam filters; however this is not guaranteed to be the case in all circumstances.

These services also give you the ability to produce professional looking HTML formatted email in record time. Additionally, they have great tools to help you easily manage your database of recipients (also referred to as subscribers) and schedule your email communications in advance.

For all these reasons, it is highly recommend that you utilize an online email marketing service as part of your Internet Marketing Strategy.

Opt-in versus Complied Email Lists

As mentioned earlier, well planned email campaigns will have an approximate delivery rate of 56 percent, out of which about 13 percent of the readers will take the next step towards making a purchase.

Email campaigns which follow closely to these statistics do so because the people they are marketing to (the people on their mailing list) have given the business permission to send them email. In other words, they have opted to receive the messages.

This is an important factor to be aware of as you implement email marketing into your strategy. Using the "opt-in" tactic is by far the best way to build a list which you can regularly market to and receive top results.

There are many list services available through which you can purchase any quantity of email address you desire and start marketing to them right away. The drawback to using "Compiled Lists" is they are just that, a list of email addresses which has been complied through various resources (such as phonebooks and online directories) and therefore may not be good prospects for your business.

Although the quantity of a complied list may be great, the quality of the list in most cases is going to be poor at best, which means your return may not be able to justify the expense of the list.

With this in mind, it is important to develop a strategy for not only how you will use email to market to your list, but how you will get people onto you list.

Successful email marketers typically have one or more ways a person can "opt-in" to their email list. In many cases this is done by giving away a report, an audio or video, a trial to their service or product, or other value-rich information in exchange for the person's email address and permission to put them on their mailing list.

Another strategy that works well for the marketer who is just getting started and has a small list (or none at all) is to partner with someone who does. This typically only works when the two businesses truly complement each other in the products and services they offer.

When you are developing your Internet Marketing Strategy, make sure you develop and add a sound opt-in approach into your plan as this will have a huge impact on the long-term internet marketing capabilities of your business.

What Every Internet Marketing Strategy Should Have

Although the following items are not on the "Must Have" list, they should all be considered as part of a well-rounded Internet Marketing Strategy.

The philosophy: Give your business every possible opportunity to succeed now and in the future.

The following components will help you do just that; they give you a way to expand your internet presence and allow your business to be found online no matter <u>where</u> people are looking for the products and services you offer.

Online Article Marketing

In the grand scheme, Article Marketing is a very effective "stealth" type of advertising for your products, services and business.

Let's begin with the basics. Here are a few guidelines which the format of your articles should follow to yield the best results from your effort.

First, articles are not purely "advertisements" and must not be written that way. Second, they should always provide value to the reader. Typically articles inform, show how to do something and/or help solve a problem. Third, each article should revolve around one specific topic. Fourth, each article should contain keyword search terms related to the subject.

Although your articles can be any length, ideally the article body should be between 600 and 1200 words. You should also consider having your articles professionally proofread as they will be a representation of you and your business which will live on the internet forever.

Once completed, articles are published in a no-cost online article directory. Articles can be submitted to multiple article directories however most search engines filter duplicate content to prevent it from appearing multiple times in their search results. It's recommended that you publish your articles to at least the top 3 directories that carry articles based on your subject matter.

Along with publishing your article, you also get to include a Resource Box. This is about two to three sentences in length and can contain a brief bio, contact information, a way to subscribe to your newsletter and/or a link to your website. In many cases you can have a different Resource Box for different article topics.

How and Why It Works

The top article directories receive a high volume of traffic and are considered authority sites by search engines. In most cases, they also rank your article within their community therefore the more relevant your articles are to the topic the better they will be ranked, and in turn read.

When someone performs a search, whether it is through a search engine or directly on the article directory website, the most relevant information for the keyword search term used is displayed. If your articles are written and optimized with this in mind, then they are likely to show up in the top of the search results and be read.

In addition to people reading your articles, directories also help you get your articles (which includes your resource box) distributed to news sources and people/businesses looking to publish fresh content on their website or blog.

Well-written focused articles have a huge potential to increase your credibility within the marketplace and have you be seen as the industry expert, as well as help you attract new clients.

Additionally, articles (and authors) are often syndicated and published on multiple websites automatically. This can highly streamline the process of getting your content out and read by the right audience.

A detailed, ongoing Article Marketing plan should be included in every Internet Marketing Strategy because of its potential to reach and connect with new people. The power of this technique is more applicable to a long-term marketing strategy rather than short. A well thought out, engaging article you write today can connect you with new prospective clients this month, next month, next year, five years from now, and so on. The possibilities are limitless.

Ways to Write Articles

To be highly effective, your Article Market plan should be consistent and intentional. Writing and publishing one article a month is a good place to start.

So, what if you are not a writer? Or, don't have the time and energy to do it. How can you benefit from this marketing strategy?

Simple; hire someone to assist you. There are a number of websites, affordable article writing services and Virtual Assistances (VAs)

available to do the bulk of the work. In addition to doing the writing, they can research topics to write on, find keyword search terms and handle getting your articles uploaded to the online directories.

I also suggest you have your helper write a draft of the article and then you review and edit it to add your "voice" or personal touch. This method can help you get many high-quality articles written in a very short period of time with minimal expense and stress.

To reiterate, articles inform, show how to do something and/or help solve a problem so these are the areas you want to key in on. Visit some of the popular online directories and investigate what other are doing to reach your market; then decide on the best strategy for you and your business.

Online Video

Like any form of marketing, Online Video allows you to showcase your products and services by using short, attractive and educational videos. It is yet another powerful way to use the internet to spread awareness to prospective customers about your business.

The main benefit of video is, unlike reading text where a potential client has to comprehend and decipher the message being conveyed, video can reach out and grab the viewer's attention in a matter of seconds, and keep them focused on the desired outcome.

And, with the advances in technology currently available, making videos and posting them online is fairly inexpensive. In addition, as with online articles, videos can help you be seen as an expert in your field, and in the same regard, they also remain on the internet forever. This means, you can invest your marketing dollars once and your video could still be getting watched (and driving prospects your way) for years to come.

In addition, another important point to note is video and Social Media go hand-in-hand because the social media sites permit their users to easily post and share video. With a well defined Online Video strategy, the possibilities to become known and expand your market share are virtually endless.

Search Engines Like Video

Another great advantage to using online video, which is still mostly untapped, is search engines (in particular Google) blend their organic webpage search results with their video results. For the marketer, this means a video search result included with a standard text search is more likely (statistics show up to 50 times more likely) to get listed on the first page of the search engine results.

This alone should inspire you to develop and implement your Online Video Marketing strategy right away. But, use caution. As with all the components of your Internet Marketing Strategy, it's important all the bases are covered.

Your video does not have to be an enormous production of epic proportions, but it must be done right and setup correctly on a video hosting website (like YouTube) for you to truly reap the benefits.

Again, like articles, videos should be based on keyword specific search terms and those keywords should be used to promote the video through the video hosting website channel, in your newsletters and on your website.

Furthermore, the video itself should be scripted to be visually appealing, recorded so it can be clearly seen and heard, and follow a logical sequence which leads the viewer to take the specific action you want them to perform at the end of the video.

It does not have to be expensive, but it does have to look (and sound) as professional as your budget allows. Make every effort to do this right so you can, again, give your business every possible opportunity to succeed now and in the future.

Mobile Website

In very simple terms, a Mobile Website is a "lighter" more basic version of one's main website which has been optimized for use by a mobile device such as a Smartphone or Tablet (iPad).

Why You Need One

The reason for having a mobile site is mobile devices, which have access the internet, outnumber desktop computers and laptops twenty to one. This means, more than ever before, people have the ability to search the web while away from their computer.

The problem is, the technology on mobile devices have underlying limitations which make a standard webpage very slow to load. In addition, the screen size of a mobile device also makes viewing a non-mobile site difficult as it involves a lot of scrolling.

The solution is to have a parallel website which provides better functionality and faster access to the mobile user. It also means savvy internet marketers (in many industries) can target mobile device users with a marketing message geared just for them.

Overall, having a mobile website gives you a greater potential to reach people who are already looking for your products and services by providing them the optimal way to find you, based on the device they are using.

Another factor to consider is in many instances, the mobile user is looking for what they want because they are ready to take action right then and there. Having your business address and phone number at their finger tips in an instant may be the deciding factor for them to select your business.

To sum it up, having a mobile website can improved discoverability of your business, give you a real advantage over competitors, expand your reach to new customers, give you the ability to better engage customers 24 hours a day and quickly position you as a market leader in your industry.

Internet Radio and Podcasts

Since its inception in 1891, the radio has been a popular form of communication and advertising media. Today, through the power of the internet, Internet Radio and Podcasting are additional ways you can speak to and connect with your audience.

Internet Radio

As you may have guessed, Internet Radio is simply a radio broadcast which takes place via the internet rather than airwaves. The requirements for listening to an Internet Radio broadcast are an internet connection and a computer or Internet Radio device.

An Internet Radio broadcast can be live (streamed over the internet in real-time) or it can be recorded and played over the internet at a predetermined time; just like radio transmitted over the airwaves.

In addition, live broadcasts can be recorded and then replayed at a later time at the discretion of the listener. Typically each radio show will be recorded and put into a library where the listen can pick and choose which broadcast/topic they would like to listen to. In addition, the recorded segments can be paused, stopped and replayed as the listener desires.

Podcasts

The main distinction between Internet Radio and a Podcast is the latter is downloaded rather than streamed live. A podcast can be a recorded version of a radio show, a recorded interview or a segment made with the intention of having listeners download and play it at their convenience.

How They Bring You Customers

The greatest benefit of hosting a radio show or developing a regular series of podcasts is it gives your prospective customers and clients another way to connect with you and the values you represent. It's another way you can build rapport with your target audience.

The best part is, you can host a regular show for free using your phone and a computer; visit www.blogtalkradio.com for the details. And, because you "run the show" you control the topics and the content.

Some of the benefits to hosting your own show are:

* You'll be seen as a leader in your community
* You'll have a platform for interacting directly with customers
* You'll increase your opportunities to meet potential partners who can help grow your business

- You can interview industry experts and gain first-hand knowledge
- You'll have the potential to reach a national (even global) audience
- You'll be seen as an expert in your field

Remember, people do business with people they know and trust and Internet radio is an exceptional way for you to do just that.

By having your own show, and speaking on what you are most passionate about in regards to your business, you'll be making a solid connection with the listening audience while building lasting relationships.

Pay-Per-Click Advertising

Pay-Per-Click (PPC) is a form of internet advertising where the advertiser pays the hosting website (the website displaying the ad) a fee when a visitor clicks on their ad, at which time the visitor is directed to a page on the advertiser's website.

Ads are setup based on keyword search terms. The advertiser sets the maximum they are willing to pay when someone clicks their ad and this, along with the relevance of the ad text to the keyword search term, determines the position the ad is placed on the search results page.

On Google, for instance, the PCP ads are always shown on the right side on the page and frequently above the organic search terms. The red outline in the picture below indicates the placement of the PCP ads.

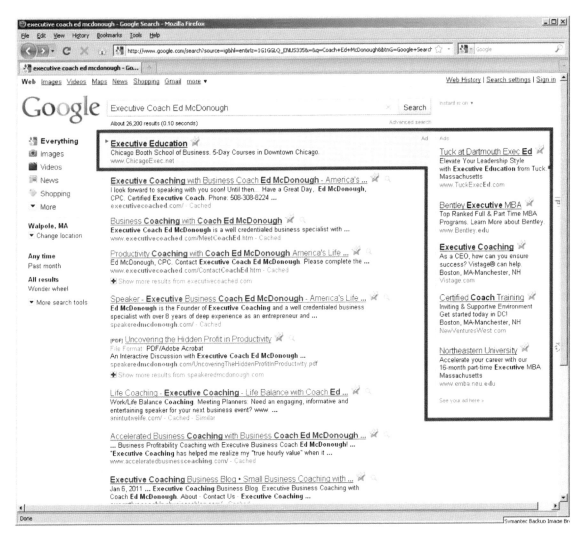

The actual fee paid by the advertiser is based on several factors which vary from one hosting website to another (i.e. Google, Yahoo, Bing, Facebook, et cetera). Typically, the more one is willing to pay to have a visitor click on their ad, the more likely the ad will be displayed on the first page of the search results. But, it's important to keep in mind that the relevance of the ad text to the keyword search term is also a factor in the ad placement.

Advantages of Pay-Per Click Advertising

First, as the advertiser, it's important to note the PCP fee is paid regardless of the action taken once the visitor reaches your website. Therefore, it is important to develop a complete PCP strategy which will yield a solid return on your investment.

The main advantage of using a Pay-Per-Click campaign is within a matter of minutes (via Google AdWords – their PCP platform) you can drive quality, targeted traffic to your website. In addition, you can schedule when and how often your ads run, set a daily budget and track the results so you know what the acquisition cost is for a new customer or lead.

Furthermore, you can run several PCP campaigns at once for various niches (products or services) within your market. Campaigns can be run locally, national or worldwide as you see fit. In many cases, you can also select a certain demographic to target with a specific ad or set of ads.

In summary, PCP ads allow you to put the message you want in front of your target audience anytime you want. No other form of advertising is this specific and effective.

Due to the flexibility of running the ads along with the speed at which you can drive targeted traffic to your website (and measure the results), Pay-Per Click Advertising is a serious form of advertising to consider as part of your overall internet marketing strategy.

A Proactive, Intentional and Consistent Plan

Like **any** effective, successful and profitable marketing strategy, Internet Marketing requires more than identifying the need for the various marketing components and then implementing them.

It requires the development of a <u>solid</u>, <u>reliable</u>, <u>proactive</u>, <u>intentional</u> and <u>consistent</u> plan be done **first**; a plan which will clearly illustrate the value it will *continually* bring to your business.

So, I challenge you to use this guide as a tool for developing your plan to increase the presence of your business on the internet. Here is my suggestion to get you started:

> **First,** decide how you will implement <u>all</u> the strategies in the section "***What Every Internet Marketing Strategy Must Have***" and WHEN they will be completed.

> **Second,** determine how often you will update your Social Media and Blogging, and develop a simple yet effective Email Marketing strategy. Put it into a written schedule which is easy for you to follow.

> **Third,** select the marketing components from the section "***What Every Internet Marketing Strategy Should Have***" and create a schedule of when they will be implemented, as well as when you will add new content to each of them. Put this into the written schedule.

> **Forth,** make sure your plan is consistent and ongoing. If you are planning on making money with your business day after day, week after week, month after month and year after year, then your marketing strategy must be a **continuous process**.

> **Five,** always remember: To be competitive and grow (or sustain) your business, Marketing never stops!

When You Feel Overwhelmed

I frequently speak with business owners who are overwhelmed with the concept of marketing on the internet. For most, a sound marketing strategy isn't something they can scratch out on the back of a napkin in an hour or two because of all the components involved.

If it seems like a daunting task to you, then the best strategy is to get help. As someone who regularly helps business owners define, implement and manage their Internet

Marketing Strategy, I understand the importance of having the right people in place to make the project effective, worthwhile and flow seamlessly.

Doing all the work yourself in most cases is not the best approach to growing your business this way. You are an expert at what you do and you're probably not an expert at marketing, and/or marketing via the internet.

When needed, and when feeling overwhelmed, look to the experts to help you. Develop a sound strategy that will bring you a return on your investment. Take part in managing and performing the tasks you enjoy, and then hire the rest out. You'll be happier and your business will be healthier and more profitable.

About the Author

Executive Coach Ed McDonough is a well credentialed business specialist with over 9 years of deep experience as an entrepreneur and successful multi-business owner.

In addition to his business owner experience, Mr. McDonough spent over 25 years as a top-level Information Technology professional and Project Management Consultant in Corporate America, making him well versed in all facets of the business environment.

His real-world brick and mortar business experience combined with his passion for internet marketing has lead him to coach business owners throughout North America to succeed from the ground up.

Mr. McDonough is also a certified as a Productivity Coach through the National Association of Productivity Coaches. He regularly helps business owners accomplish more, earn more and free-up time to do the things which are most important to them through his exclusive Productivity Intensive.

Active in the local business community, Ed is an experienced speaker who is engaging, informing, entertaining and educating. He tells it like it is and passionately shares his knowledge and real life business experiences with an open heart.

Through his speaking, he'll motivate and captivate you to do business better by showing you the way and simply encouraging you to always "do your best".

In addition to being an accomplished entrepreneur and business owner, Ed is also a certified meditation instructor and a certified Qigong (chee gung) instructor. Ed lives and practices the life balance methods he openly shares with others on a daily basis. His life is grounded and centered in the belief that anyone can accomplish anything they want when they possess the correct skills and use them wisely.

Coach Ed currently works with clients on an individual basis and he also leads groups and virtual-classes on a variety of productivity, personal development and life transformation subjects.

He helps business owners free-up their time and increase their profitability by developing, implementing and managing their Internet Marketing Strategy programs.

Ed has recently been interviewed on the television program the Psychic Holistic Spotlight, Healthy Living Radio (WAD 95.9 FM), WRNI - Rhode Island's National Public Radio, WDIS

Talk Radio and the cable television business program Process for Profit: Steps to Business Success.

Ed is available to host and participate in other like-minded educational programs involving bettering one's self and business, and may be available as a keynote speaker for your group or organization.

How to Contact Coach Ed:

Phone: **508-308-8224**

Website: **www.ExecutiveCoachEd.com**

The Complete Internet Marketing Strategy Guide

By Executive Business Coach Ed McDonough

Get the digital version of this guide online at:
www.CompleteInternetMarketingStrategy.com

Made in the USA
Charleston, SC
15 February 2011